I and You and and Don't Forget Who

What Is a Pronoun?

To my sister Maggie, who is
very much a word person.
—B.P.C.

To Wendy
—B.G.

Pronoun:
A word that
takes the place
of a noun.

NOTE: Some of the pronouns in this book are not printed in color. As each kind of pronoun is discussed, color type highlights only the corresponding pronouns. Can you find all of the pronouns?

I and You and and Don't Forget Who

What Is a Pronoun?

by Brian P. Cleary

illustrated by Brian Gable

M̲ MILLBROOK PRESS / MINNEAPOLIS

a **pronoun** steps in as a sub for a noun,

becoming the star of the feature.

Pronouns can save us
a boatload of words
and help to avoid repetition.

Without them we'd say, "Anne's father surprised Anne and bought Anne a sporty new truck."

Anne got so excited
that when Anne first saw it,

Anne couldn't believe
Anne's good luck."

Now, Anne is a really big fan of her name,

but even she'd have to agree.

These phrases could
sure use a "her"
here and there,

and perhaps an occasional "she."

"Personal pronouns"
stand in for a noun,

like Mrs. McKinley or Grady.

He could be Steven,
I might mean Josh,

they could be
Bonnie
and Brady.

"Demonstrative pronouns"
help point something out,

as in
this, these,
and **those**
are all yours.

as in someone around here is quite a good cook,

and something in here smells terrific.

Everyone, none, several, somebody, some, both, neither, nobody, many.

If it helps form a question, it's called "interrogative"— a very inquisitive pronoun.

What are you looking at?
Who is your daddy?

Which road do we take
to the hoedown?

So like a pinch hitter
Or a good baby-sitter,

the pronoun will say,
"You can go noun!
I've got your job covered."

So, what is a pronoun?

Do you know?

ABOUT THE AUTHOR & ILLUSTRATOR

BRIAN P. CLEARY is the author of the best-selling Words Are CATegorical® series as well as the Math Is CATegorical®, Food Is CATegorical™, Adventures in Memory™, and Sounds Like Reading® series. He has also written Six Sheep Sip Thick Shakes: And Other Tricky Tongue Twisters, The Punctuation Station, and several other books. Mr. Cleary lives in Cleveland, Ohio.

BRIAN GABLE is the illustrator of many Words Are CATegorical® books and the Math Is CATegorical® series. Mr. Gable also works as a political cartoonist for the Globe and Mail newspaper in Toronto, Canada.

Millbrook Press
A division of Lerner Publishing Group, Inc.
241 First Avenue North
Minneapolis, MN 55401 U.S.A.

Website address: www.lernerbooks.com

Library of Congress Cataloging-in-Publication Data

Cleary, Brian P., 1959—
    I and you and don't forget who : what is a pronoun? / by Brian P. Cleary; illustrations by Brian Gable.
        p.   cm. — (Words are categorical)
    Summary: Rhyming text and illustrations of comical cats present numerous examples of pronouns and their functions, from "he" and "she" to "anyone," "neither," and "which."
    ISBN-13: 978-1-57505-596-1 (lib. bdg. : alk. paper)
    ISBN-10: 1-57505-596-1 (lib. bdg. : alk. paper)
    1. English language—Pronoun—Juvenile literature. [1. English language—Pronoun.] I. Gable, Brian, 1949— ill. II. Title. III. Series.
PE1261.C58 2004
428.2—dc21   2003001712
                                                                              •

Manufactured in the United States of America
10 — DP — 2/1/12